Ghosts Monsters and Legends

Written by Susannah Bradley
Illustrated by Barrie Appleby

Henderson
Woodbridge, England *Publishing*

Frankenstein's Monster

Most people have heard of this monster, if they haven't heard of any others. The story is nearly two hundred years old, because it was written in the early nineteenth century by Mary Shelley, the wife of Percy Shelley, the English poet. Her character, Dr Frankenstein, was an inventor who pottered about at home, trying to make a human person out of human sections and electricity. Into this creation goes the brain of a murderer, and during an electrical storm the creature comes to life. It is then that Dr Frankenstein realises that he has created something outside his control — the human being he has made is a terrifying monster.

This story was first made into a film in 1931, but since then Frankenstein's monster has been used by many different film-makers to frighten us into jelly. The story of how the chained monster breaks out and terrifies everyone has become a classic.

The Loch Ness Monster

The stretch of water known as Loch Ness, in the north of Scotland, has been the location for one of the most baffling of all monster mysteries. A huge, serpent-like monster is said to live here, and it has been hunted by some very determined people. All the same, there is still no real proof that it exists. Photographs could be fakes, or just not clear enough.

The first person to write about this monster was St Columba — and if you can't trust the word of a saint, whose word can you trust? He was out in the Scottish Highlands doing his work as a Christian missionary near Loch Ness one day in the 6th century when he met some people who were burying a man killed by a monster in the loch. One of St Columba's companions swam out to retrieve the dead man's boat, and was himself chased by the monster. St Columba made the sign of the Cross at it and shooed it away. There were more reported sightings of it down the centuries, but it is only in this century that looking for it has become such an absorbing pastime. The monster is said to be about 9 metres long with several humps — but even the sonar equipment used to monitor it cannot come up with any real proof.

The Minotaur

The Minotaur was a horrible creature in Greek mythology. It had the head and horns of the white bull which was its father, and the body of a human, because its mother was the Queen of Crete. It was so horrible to look at that the queen had a maze constructed for it to live in, known as the labyrinth. As it would eat nothing but humans, people were sent in to provide food for it. Every spring, seven youths and seven maidens arrived as food for the Minotaur in a ship with black sails. They came by order of the ruler of Crete, King Midas, who had powers over their homeland of Athens. This sacrifice was the only way that the Athenian people could keep King Midas's armies from wrecking their country.

Theseus, son of the Athenian King, Aegeus, had been abroad when this sacrifice was first arranged. When he returned he was appalled at this waste of young life and insisted on going with the next boat to Athens, hoping to kill the monster. His father was distraught, but had to allow his son to go. He only asked that, should Theseus manage to kill the monster, the sails of the boat should be changed to white, so that he could see at once that his son was safe.

When Theseus and the other young people arrived in Crete, Ariadne, daughter of King Midas, immediately fell in love with him. Determined to save him from the Minotaur, she gave him a magic sword and a ball of wool. Fastening one end of the wool to the labyrinth's entrance, Theseus unravelled it as he went along. In the centre he met the Minotaur, killed it with the magic sword, and retraced his steps, guided by the wool, to a joyful Ariadne. Taking her with them, all the young Athenians set sail once more for home — but as they had forgotten to change the sail, King Aegeus believed his son to be dead. He threw himself into the sea and drowned — and to this day, that sea bears his name — the Aegean.

Cyclops

Not just one monster here, but a whole race of them. The Cyclops were a race of one-eyed giants who inhabited an island where they kept sheep, we are told in the myths of Ancient Greece.

Odysseus, the Greek warrior, found his ship blown off-course on his return from the Trojan wars. He and his shipmates were washed up on the island of the Cyclops. Not realising their danger, they began to explore, and had just come across a cave stocked with food when the largest Cyclops of all, Polyphemus, returned with his sheep. He drove the sheep into the cave and ate two of

Odysseus's men for supper; then he shut the rest of the men in the cave with the sheep, ignoring their pleas for food and shelter.

Odysseus and his friends sharpened a huge pole into a point.

Polyphemus returned and ate another two men, but as he fell asleep afterwards, Odysseus and his men plunged the sharpened pole into his eye. Blind, and roaring with rage, the Cyclops blundered about the cave, and when he went out with his sheep he was unable to see that his visitors were clinging on to the sheep's bellies. They escaped to their ship, taking some of the sheep with them for food.

The Gorgons

Three terrible women, with hair made of snakes, were monsters of Greek myth. Medusa was the most terrible of the three. She had once been a beautiful girl, but had boasted that she was lovelier even than the goddess Athene — so Athene had changed her and her sisters into hideous creatures so ghastly that anyone looking at them immediately turned to stone.

The Greek hero, Perseus, went on a mission to kill Medusa. Armed with a curved sword, a magic goat-skin bag and a helmet which made him invisible, he set off. Hermes, the messenger of the gods, gave him a pair of winged sandals to make transport easier, and he also took a mirror, to save having to look directly at Medusa. After all this preparation he was lucky enough to find Medusa asleep. With his sword he cut off her head, while the snakes writhed and hissed at him. He put Medusa's head in the goat-skin bag and escaped from the other Gorgons because he was invisible.

OTHER MONSTERS

The Makara
This name means 'sea monster' and it describes creatures in Buddhist and Hindu religions which are half-fish and half-mammal.

A Hindu one has the head of an elephant, the body of a tortoise and the tail of a fish, which contains a scorpion's sting. Ganga, goddess of the Holy River Ganges, is said to have ridden down the river on this beast, spreading fertility and good fortune.

Kujata
This huge bull with 4,000 eyes, ears, nostrils, mouths and feet comes from ancient Moslem mythology. It would take 500 years to travel from one eye to another! A ruby on Kujata's back is the platform for an angel to stand on to reach our earth.

T'ao T'ien
This is a Chinese monster, one of four sent into outer darkness by the Emperor Shun about 4,000 years ago. It has two bodies, one to the left and one to the right of its face, which may look like that of a dragon, a tiger or a man. Chinese plates sometimes show this horrible creature, whose name means 'greedy glutton', as a reminder not to eat too much.

The Basilisk

Not all monsters have to be vast! The Basilisk was less than 60 cm long but for all that it was deadly. Its poisonous breath killed all plant life except the rue, and a glance from it could kill any creature (except the weasel) or shatter boulders. There could be any amount of Basilisks lurking around the next corner, for it was hatched from an egg laid by an elderly cockerel on a dung-heap — and in the 15th century people truly believed that such a thing was possible. Basilisks had pointed wings and a yellow tail curled over its back, a cockerel's head and toad-like red eyes. It formed deserts in which to live, and if you planned to cross a desert you were wise to take with you a weasel crowing cock, because these were the only creatures it feared. Failing that, a mirror could be held up to it for it to be slain by the horror of its own reflection.

MAKING A DRAGON MASCOT

All you need for this is a cardboard carton, some scissors, and drawing and painting materials. You don't need to be all that good at drawing, because dragons can look like whatever you choose — so however your mascot turns out, tell people that's how you meant it to be.

1. *Copy the body piece, but make it much bigger. Make sure the bottom edge is flat. Cut it out. Snip along lines A, B and C.*

2. *Copy the leg pieces. The most important thing is to make the slit in the centre of the legs the same length as the space between the end of the lines A and B, and the base. When you have cut them out and made the slits at points D and E, fit them on to the body.*

3. *Copy the wing piece. Again, make the slit (F) the same length as the space between the end of line C and the base. Cut out, and snip up line F. Fold back the wings along the dotted lines. Insert into Slot C.*

4. *Take it all apart again and paint it.*

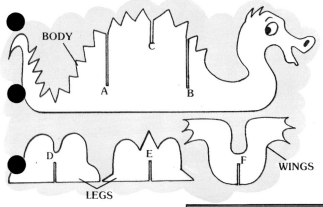

BODY

A

C

B

D

E

F

WINGS

LEGS

CROSSWORD PUZZLE

Across
1. All the better for seeing you with
6. Feeling of excitement
7. Time when darkness falls
8. Good luck token, or spell
10. Source of light in the night sky
12. What makes a ghost clank
14. Frog-like creature
15. Bone of the head
17. Move softly and slowly
18. State of utter fright
19. Witch's pet

Down
2. Just bones
3. Not fat
4. Fairy circle
5. Bewitching
9. Witchcraft
10. Face disguise
11. Shape of a skull
13. Blood-sucking ghoul
15. Ghost
16. Opposite of dark

Answers appear on page 48

APPLE GAMES

The Romans had a festival called 'Pomona' to encourage the apple crop to grow. They believed that if they did this, the gods would be pleased enough to grant them a large harvest. Even today we play apple games like those on these pages.

Bob Apple

Half fill a bowl of water and put it on the floor — somewhere which can be easily mopped up afterwards.

Choose about twelve apples, and make a slit in each one, just large enough to insert a small coin. Wedge one into each apple — use coins of different values. Each player has to throw lots to decide who goes first and then each one in turn has to try to pick up an apple from the bowl using only his or her teeth. Everybody gets very wet and whoever gets the apple with the most valuable coin is, of course, the winner.

Snap Apple

Thread apples on to strings and suspend them from a high point over a door frame. Then see who can eat one quickest — without touching them with your hands!

Tapping the Trees

Even today, some apple-growers go round their orchards at New Year or some other time, tapping the trunks of the trees to bring good luck on the next crop.

OOCH!

TAP!

Love-apples

Did you know that tomatoes used to be called 'love-apples'? Centuries ago, people thought that eating them was bound to make you fall in love. A rumour caught on that love-apples were poisonous, and it was hundreds of years before someone took the risk of eating some. Then it was discovered that they were safe to eat — and we have eaten them ever since.

Apple Pips

If a girl wants to know which of her sweethearts to marry, she should stick an apple pip on her cheek for each one of her boyfriends. The one which falls off last is the one she should wed! If any girl is tempted to try it, she should say:

'Pippin, pippin, I stick thee there,
If he is true, you must declare.'

Ancient apples

The Druids, people who lived in Ancient Britain, believed in a magic land called Avalon, where apples grew in plenty and immortal souls lived. In Cornwall at Hallowe'en it is considered lucky to put an apple under your pillow; you can dream a wish, then, eat the apple in the morning.

Apple Peel

To find out who your true love is, peel an apple so that it comes off in an unbroken piece, and then throw the peel over your right shoulder. When you turn around you should see the peel in the shape of your true love's initial.

FAIRIES

How would you describe a fairy? Probably as something as tiny as your hand, who dances prettily in a dress as delicate as a spider's web and flits about the bottom of people's gardens with the sun sparkling on her wings. But it hasn't always been like that.

In olden times people believed that fairies might be as big as themselves, and there was nothing harmless or attractive about them. It was thought that fairies could bring all kinds of misfortune, from turning the milk sour to swapping babies for their own nasty offspring.

Fairyland was located underground or in dense woodland. A queen ruled there, and sometimes a king, too. Even in the earliest accounts, much dancing and singing was thought to go on in fairy life. Fairies were thought to be the ghosts of babies who had died before being christened, or of grown people who had never had the chance of being converted to Christianity.

There are two main groups of fairies: the hobgoblins who live in houses and help (unless anyone offends them) with the housework, and outdoor creatures such as pixies, boggarts, elves and leprechauns who make their homes in woods and marshes.

Generally, fairies are thought to be helpful, if mischievous creatures, who may be very skilled at certain jobs like tin-mining, tailoring or shoeing horses. They are greedy for gold, and often bad-tempered; but then, so are many other people!

THE MISCHIEVOUS LITTLE GIRL

In 1967 two small boys lived with their parents in a house in Oundle, Northamptonshire, England. Their father had been altering a wall in the house when their mother began to notice that things were being moved. At first she scolded the boys for it but each time they protested that they had not done it. Finally, when half a cucumber was found on a shelf over a door, their mother began to think that a mischievous spirit must be present in the house. As the weeks went by she noticed that the things which were moved were always from the kitchen — little things which were either pretty or edible.

At the time she was expecting a visit from her aunt, whom she had not seen for many years. Not having much money to buy an expensive present, she decided to paint a picture for her. The idea of a little girl in 19th century dress presented itself to her, and she set to work on the painting in good time for her aunt's visit. Yet when the aunt arrived she had to admit that she would have liked even more time to get it right; even after repainting the face three times, the little girl appeared to have a crooked lip.

The aunt was delighted with the painting, despite the girl's lip, and took it with her when she left. But on the night before she departed a strange thing happened. One of the boys had woken up and he and his mother had come downstairs to get him a drink. As they sat in the darkened living-room the figure of a young girl appeared near the place in the wall which had been altered. Almost immediately she vanished, but it was long enough for them to see that she was exactly like the girl in the painting — even down to the crooked lip . . .

THE JOURNEY OF PEGASUS

Pegasus was a mythical winged horse. See if you can help him to fly across the galaxy by starting at the right letter in our network of stars and moving in order through the letters of Jupiter, Pluto, Mars and Venus.

THE FROG BOX

Can you draw three straight lines so that there are seven compartments, each with three frogs in it?

Answers appear on page 48

MAKING A GHOSTLY PEEP SHOW

You'll need:
a shoe box
five pieces of
strong card
sheet of
grease-proof paper
pencil
paints
scissors

What you are going to do is to make a sort of three-D picture, so draw out a plan first on the grease-proof paper. The scene could be of a ghostly cave, with monsters and bats peeping out from the sides. Have at least four sections. Each section, made of card, has a hole in it. The holes should all be different sizes. The first one should be small and round. The next one should be quite big and jagged. Others should get smaller until the last one has no hole in it at all. This one is the backdrop.

Draw the back of the cave on the backdrop. It can be horrible, with old skeletons hanging from hooks in the wall, or cobwebs covering old books.

The card in front of the backdrop should show the most important details — Dracula rising from a tomb, a ghost flitting past, or something like that. Do more spiders' webs at the sides, or a bat or two.

The remaining scenes can have fern fronds and snakes, and other creepy things around the edges. If you want some of these things to come over the jagged edges of the central hole, cut some out and stick them on.

Make slits in the shoe box at regular intervals and slot the cards in, with the backdrop at the far end and the small-holed card at the front. When you are happy with the arrangement, take all the cards out again and paint them.

Then put them back and let all your friends peep through the little hole at the spooky scene.

WITCH'S GAME

This game makes you shudder!

Prepare a shallow cardboard box of the following:

* a cling-film parcel of some cold cooked marrow or pumpkin
* a black olive with the stone removed
* some cold, cooked spaghetti
* some cold, cooked pasta twirls or macaroni
* a cold, cooked sausage with one end broken off
* a rubber or surgical glove, smeared with washing-up liquid

You need a lot of people to play this game, to get the most fun out of it. The box of items is hidden by the person organising the game. This person should have a helper to make sure the game runs smoothly.

All the players sit around the edges of the room in a circle, so that there is plenty of room for the organisers to circulate in the middle. Everyone, except the organisers, is blindfolded — and when this has been done, the organiser brings out the box of horrible things.

"I'm sorry we've had to blindfold you," announces the organiser. "but we have discovered something too terrible to look at. We have here the contents of a witch's pantry. The witch herself is dead so we can't ask her what everything is, so that is why we are asking you. Please tell us what you think each thing is. Be brave. See who dares to touch all six horrible things in our box."

Then let each person feel the contents of the box. The organiser should first have cut a hole in the base or side of the box, through which the rubber or surgical glove is pushed. With the organiser's hand lying limply inside it and occasionally twitching, a lot of fun can be had. The assistant should write down what each person thinks each item is. It improves the game if the organisers have thought up some horrible suggestions for the things to mention as they are being handled, like the following:

- cling-filmed marrow or pumpkin — skinned toad, bat's droppings
- black olive — bat's droppings, sparrow's heart, person's eyeball
- spaghetti — boiled worms, eels' backbones, human brains
- pasta twirls or macaroni — dead maggots, twisted slugs
- sausage — human finger
- glove — severed hand which still twitches

The organiser can say things like: "Did you put in the thing we thought was a frog's leg?"

To which the assistant can reply: "You mean the things like dead maggots? Yes — there they are, now, look."

When everyone has had a go at everything, the blindfolds are removed and the true identities of the items can be revealed. Try thinking up your own horrible things to put in the box — they should be quite harmless, but lots of fun will be had.

DRAGONS

Eastern Dragons are very different from Western ones. In the East — mainly in China — dragons may be mischievous, but they are thought to be good creatures at heart. In the West the legends about them show them to be wicked monsters, to be fought and destroyed.

Throughout history both kinds of dragon have been respected and feared for the powers they possess.

Typical Western Dragon

Size:	Huge
Head:	Serpent-like
Colour:	Variable
Body:	Scaly, with wings
Tail:	Long, thin and spiked
Mouth:	Breathing fire
Home:	Cave, with hidden chambers full of fabulous piles of gold and jewels
Nature:	Aggressive
Hobbies:	Fighting, carrying off maidens, and getting more treasure

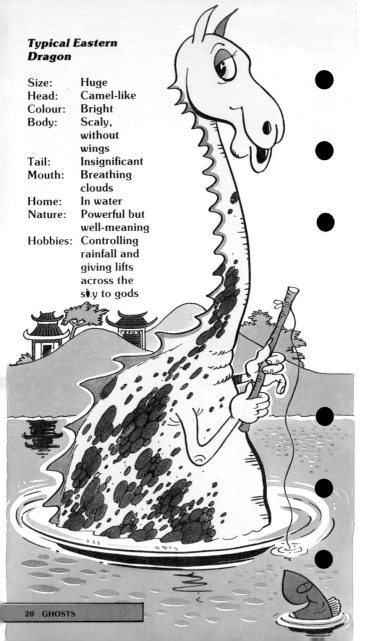

Typical Eastern Dragon

Size:	Huge
Head:	Camel-like
Colour:	Bright
Body:	Scaly, without wings
Tail:	Insignificant
Mouth:	Breathing clouds
Home:	In water
Nature:	Powerful but well-meaning
Hobbies:	Controlling rainfall and giving lifts across the sky to gods

CHINESE DRAGONS

The Chinese New Year

Sometime around the end of February each year, the exact date depending on the stages of the moon, is a holiday for Chinese people. Then they celebrate the New Year and the coming of spring. A very special dragon dance is traditionally performed then. Men dressed in black carry bright lanterns of different colours, twisting and turning. In the dark the lanterns look like a dragon slithering past. This looks spectacular, but its original purpose was part of a religious ceremony to encourage crops to grow.

Rain-making

Because Chinese dragons are said to control water, carvings of dragons are often placed at the prows of boats. These ward off evil spirits. In June, Chinese boat festivals are held. This may be to encourage rain to fall on the rice crop, or it may be because of an old legend which says that a wise government official called Chu Yuan, banished by his king in the 4th century BC, returned after his death with a message for his loved ones. He told them that they should throw food wrapped in bamboo leaves into the river as sacrifices to his spirit, and scare away demons and ghosts by racing dragon-prowed boats. Dragon boat races are still held, and food is wrapped in bamboo leaves; but these days it is eaten, not thrown overboard.

The Pearl of the Dragon

Underneath the chin of a Chinese dragon is a pearl. Without it, he would lose his powers, so each dragon knows that he must look after his pearl very carefully. Nevertheless, everyone loses something valuable eventually, and one day a dragon lost his pearl. What happened to the dragon because of this has not come down to us, but the pearl was found by a poor Chinese boy who lived with his mother in great poverty. He took it home to his mother, who put it into a jar containing the few grains of rice remaining to them. Next morning the jar was full of rice to the brim, with the pearl on top. This ability of the pearl to make rice soon made their fortune; but jealous neighbours tried to steal it from them. To stop this, the boy put the pearl into his mouth, but swallowed it accidentally.

At once he was stricken with a terrible thirst. He rushed to the river, and drank it dry. His mother could only cry in terror, while the neighbours watched, amazed. In the midst of a sudden thunderstorm they saw the boy transformed into a mighty dragon, while his mother clung to him in tears. He twisted and turned, to throw her off, and as the rain refilled the river he sank into it, his mother cast on to the bank.

WESTERN DRAGONS

Welsh Dragons

All dragons are said to be rich, and Welsh ones are said to have worn gold rings in their tails. There are deposits of gold in the Welsh mountains, which are owned by the Queen; but a dragon would doubtless say that it was his by right. Welsh dragons were believed to live at the bottom of lakes, so maybe they had Chinese ancestors; they guarded wells and holy springs.

It is said that St George of England crossed into Wales for his fight with the Dragon.

Viking Dragons

Dragons were used as a symbol of war on the ships of that warrior race, the Vikings, who captured so much territory around their Scandinavian homeland. They painted dragons on their shields, too.

Pendragons

Pendragon was the name given to an English knight who had killed a chief in battle. In the legends of King Arthur's Round Table, Arthur's father was given the title Uther Pendragon, and allowed to use the symbol of a dragon on his personal standard.

St George and the Dragon

There are several versions of the story of St George and the Dragon, for the legend is so old that no one can be sure of the truth any more. It was in 1222 that St George's Day began to be commemorated on 23 April in England, with St George as a national saint.

It is thought that St George was not English at all, but was from the East. He was a hero of the Crusaders, who returned to England with stories of how he had slain a dragon. This dragon, it was said, had lived outside Silene. Every night it had climbed over the city walls, killing people with its poisonous breath before eating them. People had been too frightened to go to sleep for fear of being attacked in their beds. For a while they kept it at bay by feeding sheep to it at the rate of two a day, but when there were no more sheep, the dragon once more climbed into the city at night. Thereafter the people drew lots to determine which of them should be sacrificed to it; one person each night went out to become the dragon's dinner, while the others were able to rest easy in their beds.

When the Princess Saba, daughter of the king, became the person designated to be the next sacrifice, George decided the time had come to brave the dragon. Making the sign of the cross and breathing a prayer, he closed his visor against the dragon's poisonous breath and pierced the beast with his lance. The princess tied up the dragon with her belt and together they led the subdued beast back to the city.

The people were terrified of it, and so George cut off its head in the name of Christianity, and the whole city was converted to this religion.

SPOOKY MAZE

Find your way through this maze . . . if you can!
But try not to come face to face with any spooks!

Answer appears on page 48

MAKING CAT CAKES

Cats are magical creatures. Put their faces on these little cakes and they are sure to taste delicious!

You'll need:
75g soft margarine
75g caster sugar
75g self-raising flour
½ level teaspoon baking powder
1 egg
1 orange
1 tablespoon milk
For decorating:
175g icing sugar
small round sweets
angelica or liquorice
boot-laces
paper bun cases

Beat up the margarine with the caster sugar until it is light and fluffy. Break the egg into a cup and beat it, then add it to the mixture. Grate the orange peel finely and add it to the flour in a separate bowl, and put in the baking powder, too. Fold the flour into the sugar mixture.

Make it sloppy enough to drop off the spoon by adding the milk, and as much of the juice of the orange as you need. Line a bun tin with the paper cases. Put equal quantities of the mixture into each of the cases and bake at Gas Mark 5, 375°F, 190°C for 15-20 minutes. Get a grown-up to take them out of the cooker for you because everything wil be very hot by now.

To decorate:
When the cakes are cool, mix the icing sugar with 3 teaspoons of water. It will be stiff at first, but don't be tempted to add lots more water as it could easily end up too runny. Spread over the cakes. Before it is quite set add the face details using the round sweets for eyes and snippets of angelica or licquorice for ears, nose and whiskers.

GHOST STORY

THE PLEA FOR HELP

Ghost stories get passed from one person to another. This one appeared in *Ghosts of Fact and Fiction* by Daniel Farson.

In the ship's log of a seaborne vessel there appeared the words: 'Steer to the north-east.'

The captain had not written it, but the first mate said he thought he had seen a strange man writing something in the captain's cabin.

The captain impulsively changed course to the north-east — and they came across the survivors of a shipwreck. As they pulled the men aboard the first mate exclaimed: "That is the man I saw writing in the captain's cabin."

The sailor was asked to write the words 'Steer to the north-east' on a piece of paper — and his writing exactly matched that in the captain's log. He told them that he had gone into a trance on the night before the rescue, but awoke from it convinced that help was on its way.

WITCHES' PUZZLES

WITCHES' SAUCEPANS

The title of this puzzle is the clue to a nine-letter word which can be made from the letters in this word square. See if you can find seven three-letter words, too. You are allowed to start at any letter of your choice,

but you must not jump over any letters, although you can go in any direction — up, down, sideways or diagonally.

C	A	R
D	O	N
S	U	L

WORD LADDERS

It isn't only witches who can change things . . . you can even change black into white with this puzzle! When you have worked it out see what word ladders of your own you can invent. You must have the same number of letters in the beginning and finishing words. We tried to turn trick into treat, but it seems impossible! You might manage it, though — if you try hard enough.

BLACK

. . . . . Loose

. . . . . To make sleek

. . . . . A piece of cake

. . . . . Pungent food flavouring

. . . . . Backbone

. . . . . Glow with light

. . . . . Long complaining wail

WHITE

Answers appear on page 48

PALM READING

Add a touch of mystery to your image — try reading the palms of your friends. Don't take it too seriously — it's just a bit of fun.

The Mounts and Lines of the Hand

These are the major lines and mounts, or lumpy areas, which you find on a human hand. On some people certain lines are very faint; sometimes the lines on a person's left hand are very different from those on the right hand. This is because the dominant hand (the right hand for most of us, but the left hand for those who are left-handed) show signs of the way the owner's life is at that moment, but the other hand shows natural characteristics which that person was born with. So you should always look at both hands — and here is what to look for:

The Thumb

If the thumb curls sharply backwards at a sharp angle from the fingers, it is a sign that its owner is strong-willed. If you can easily push it backwards, that person is easily swayed by other people; if it is hard to move, it could indicate stubborness.

Some thumbs are thinner in the middle than others. This is a sign of an easy-going nature.

The Fingers

The shape of the fingers can tell you a lot about a person's character. Square fingertips indicate a practical personality. Such a person is good in a crisis, and likes to be fair.

Long, tapering fingers is a sign of artistic talent. This doesn't mean that everyone with long fingers is good at drawing — the talent could be in music, a love of reading, or being aware of other people's feelings.

Rounded fingertips are also a sign of an artistic nature, but in a less emotional way. These people are content to let other people make the headlines, and prefer to turn their artistic talents to things which are useful in everyday life.

The Lines

The Life Line: This is the major line on the hand. If it is long and deep it shows energy and enthusiasm for what is going on all around. If it is short, or weak, it means that its owner doesn't bother much about what is going on around him; he doesn't let anything worry him too much. If it is strongly curved it indicates travel to far places, but the journeys always end back at home.

The Heart Line: A long heart line, stretching right across the palm, shows a need to be liked by everyone. A short one which ends suddenly indicates that its owner is not ready to trust anyone very much. A heart line which runs into the mound under Saturn (the middle finger) belongs to someone who expects friends to be perfect . . . but a heart line which

ends in Jupiter shows a willingness to make friends with anyone who thinks you are wonderful.

The Head Line: If it forks, one section sloping downwards, be sure to point out that its owner can see both sides of an argument, and judge well. This person is a good peacemaker. A head line which runs straight across the hand shows a clear mind which thinks things out carefully. If it is crooked, its owner has to think hard about things before coming to a decision

The Fate Line: Some people have hardly any fate line at all — it doesn't mean that they have no future, though . . . just that they are unlikely to be very ambitious. A strong fate line ending in the mount of Jupiter shows that the person could be famous. If it ends in the mount of Saturn, he or she will be successful.

MAKING A PALMIST'S TENT

If you already have a tent or a playhouse, decorate the outside of it and use that; but if not, this method of making a tent will do well — and you can use it to play in at other times, too.

You'll need:
a washing line which stretches across the lawn; if your household uses a rotary clothes dryer you will have to fix up your own rope across the garden
a large blanket
several heavy stones
some card and colouring things to make a notice
a few pegs

Have the washing line quite low, so that when you throw the blanket over it the edges touch the ground on both sides.

Secure the blanket in place with the heavy stones. Use pegs to hold the back edges together, and to fasten a notice to the front telling people that this is where they can have their palms read. Then sit back inside and wait for customers!

UP IN THE AIR GHOSTS

Flight Warning

On 29 December, 1972, Eastern Airlines L-1011 Tristar crashed in Florida, killing Captain Robert Loft and Second Officer Don Repo. Some time later, on a flight to San Francisco, one of the airline's vice-presidents realised that the uniformed officer he was talking to was Captain Loft. As soon as he realised this, the Captain vanished.

Second Officer Repo appeared to a stewardess on a flight to Mexico City in February, 1974. When she told the pilot, he said that he had seen him too — and that Repo had warned him to look out for a fire on the aircraft. Later on the flight, fire did break out in one of the engines but was quickly put out, thanks to the warning.

After 1974 there were no further sightings of these two men.

Voice From the Past

In 1905 a female singer killed herself by falling through the skylight of a theatre in South London while singing loudly. Her ghost has been seen in the building several times, and there are claims that her voice has been recorded on tape.

On the Runway

As aircraft take off from London's Heathrow Airport the pilots sometimes see the figure of a man in a bowler hat. This has happened many times since a day in March, 1948, when 22 passengers, mainly businessmen, were killed as their DC3 aeroplane crashed there.

Still Flying?

In the Castle Air Force Museum in California is a wartime bomber, *Raz'n Hell*. Museum staff believe that it is haunted, because its locked doors have been known to swing open of their own accord, the landing lights have inexplicably come on, and a ghostly figure has been seen in the cockpit. Some people there believe that the dead crew of *Raz'n Hell* return to fly the aircraft.

On the High Wire

Visitors to a High Wire act in the Olympiadrome in Paris were prepared to be amazed, but they got more than they bargained for on the day that Pierre Hurette remounted the wire after a very bad accident in which his partner had been killed. He himself had suffered terrible injuries, and still had a bandaged arm and ribs — but he was determined to perform his act despite his painful injuries.

The audience held its breath as he reached the wire and began to walk across. It was obvious to everyone there that he was having difficulty in taking every step. When he reached the halfway point on the wire he appeared to stumble; it seemed inevitable that he should fall.

Then, amazingly, there appeared another figure on the wire. This second man gripped Hurette, and steadied him. He walked to the end of the wire and returned with a rope for Hurette to cling to on the remainder of the walk across the wire. By the time Hurette had climbed down to safety, the mysterious figure had gone.

Yet Hurette, and many of the audience, had recognised the man as Paul de Champ, Hurette's dead partner. Only four weeks before, he had been a living part of the high wire act — and had returned from the dead to save his old friend from the fate which had overtaken him.

The Mysterious Airman

In 1977, a Lincoln bomber underwent a programme of repair in Cosford, Shropshire, in England. Workers on the aircraft noticed an airman loitering nearby as they worked — an airman who wore the leather jacket and white polo-necked jersey of wartime air crew. They came to look upon him as a good luck charm — for when an engineer escaped unharmed from a 4.5 metre fall to a concrete wall, and someone else walked unscathed from an encounter with a sharp propeller, they felt sure that they were being protected. Although it was cold, inside the plane it was cosy enough for them to work in their shirt sleeves.

They never found out the airman's identity, but all the same, they felt sure that he was on their side.

GHOSTLY GAME

TELLING GHOST STORIES

Here's a game for a group of you to play on a dark evening — sitting round a fire with only the firelight to see by is best.

The idea is to tell a ghost story between you. One person starts, and the one next to him carries on, and so on, until someone thinks of an ending. It has to be a good ending! And the longer it can be put off, the better, so make a rule that whoever finishes the story loses a point. The winner is the person with the least points against him at the end.

When a story has ended, the person next in line has to begin the next story — not the person who ended the previous one.

Here are a few ideas for opening lines to get you going . . .

'It was a dark night when old George set out to fetch the doctor to his old master . . .'

'It seemed like a very ordinary doll when Lucy opened the parcel, but there was something strange about its eyes . . .'

'No one ever walked past The Old Grange without looking away. It was said that if you looked into its windows you could be trapped in a web of terror. But one day . . .'

'Under the root of the elder tree lived a horrible creature — just yards from a path where the children walked home from school . . .'

THE WAXWORKS HORROR

In the middle of the 19th century in Sacramento, USA, a waxworks exhibition opened to the public. The owner, Richard Turner, hoped that it would be as popular as the Madame Tussaud exhibition was in London. He had bought six French waxworks of characters awaiting execution during the French Revolution, whose faces were particularly realistic — their faces had been made from moulds pressed from actual victims after death.

These figures made the exhibition an instant success — but each morning when the doors were opened, one of them was in a different place with its head removed from its body.

Turner and the caretaker decided to spend the night in the hall to see what happened. The first time they fell asleep, but the next time the horrified men saw the figure move, and heard it tell them to leave him and his companions in peace.

They left at once in terror — but a reporter from a local newspaper begged to be allowed to spend the night in the hall. Turner reluctantly agreed, although the figure had said, in French: "Come here no more during the hours of darkness or you will regret it."

The reporter *did* regret it, for during the night the model of Nicodeme Leopold-Lepide, who had during his life helped the rich to collect taxes from the poor, began to strangle the reporter with its waxen fingers. Only when the caretaker rushed in did the reporter's terror subside.

The waxwork figure, now standing headless by the door, was found to have damaged fingers . . . and Richard Turner took the decision to have it melted down. After that, there were no more strange happenings at the exhibition.

THE ROYAL GHOSTS

Catherine Howard

Catherine Howard, the fifth wife of Henry VIII of England, soon fell out of favour, and was sentenced to death for adultery. In a last attempt to save her own life she ran through the corridors of Hampton Court Palace to the King's chambers, to plead with him to spare her life. It was no good — Catherine was executed . . . but her spirit haunts Hampton Court, for her ghost has been seen running through the corridors in her everlasting search for mercy from Henry.

Anne Boleyn

Henry's second wife, Anne Boleyn, was also beheaded, and her ghost haunts the Tower of London, where she spent her last weeks. The place where her ghost has been seen more than anywhere else is in the courtyard below her old rooms, where she paces up and down. The official guide-book to the Tower of London states that of all the Tower's ghosts, she is the one more frequently seen. Maybe it is because she so fervently protested her innocence of the charges made against her.

Boadicea

Boadicea, or Budicca, was the Queen of the Iceni tribe in East Anglia at the time of the Roman occupation of Britain. She was a warrior Queen, and finally died in battle, but her ghost rides on. Sightings of the red-haired queen, riding in her chariot, have taken place many times in Lincolnshire.

Queen Victoria

It is said that Queen Victoria's spectre walks around Osborne House on the Isle of Wight. The Queen loved Osborne — so it is likely that she is just enjoying her old home as she did when she was alive.

The Bricked-Up Door

Workmen often see ghosts — maybe because their work disturbs the buildings which contain them. In 1977, workmen at Britain's Windsor Castle saw the ghost of King Henry VIII appear to walk through a wall. Old plans showed that there had been a door there years before.

Charles I

Another ghostly inhabitant of Windsor Castle is said to be King Charles I, who was beheaded in 1649. He has often been seen standing by a table in the library there. His head is in place at Windsor; but in Maple Hall, Cheshire, it is said that the headless body of the king has been seen.

The Headless Ride

Anne Boleyn is said to ride from the Tower of London to Blickling Hall, Norfolk, on 19 May each year. She rides in a coach pulled by headless horses and driven by headless coachmen. She herself is headless, too.

George IV

King George IV built a vast, ornate palace at Brighton, known as The Pavilion. He filled it with art treasures of many kinds — and now his ghost walks through its fabulous rooms, it is said.

Jane Seymour

The third wife of Henry VIII's six wives glides around Hampton Court Palace, it is said. Jane Seymour walks on 12 October, the date on which her son, Edward VI, was born.

Elizabeth I

Several people have claimed to have seen the ghost of Good Queen Bess, Elizabeth I, in the library at Windsor Castle. She was a well-read, scholarly person, so maybe old habits die hard.

The Black Hound of Gatcombe

The Princess Royal's home, Gatcombe Park, is said to be haunted by the black hound of Odin, a Viking warrior of bygone days.

GHOSTLY CHEATS

There are a lot of ghostly tales which cannot be explained away. But there are also plenty which can.

The Photograph

Sometimes a photograph appears in the newspapers showing a ghost on it. The figure is solid enough except that whatever is behind it shows through. So how is it done?

ANSWER: If you use a very slow film it is possible to fake a ghost. If someone walks past a camera which has the shutter open to slowly take a photograph, and pauses briefly before continuing on his way, his image may show up on the print. Only, because he wasn't there all the time, whatever was behind him will also appear on the photograph . . . as if it is showing through him.

Another way of faking a photograph is to set up a model of some kind. If it is realistic enough it can fool people. This is what 13-year-old Elsie Wright and her cousin Frances did in 1917. Frances had fallen into a stream and to avoid a ticking-off, said that she had been playing with fairies. Challenged by Elsie's father to take a photograph of them, the two girls set up some amazingly detailed paper cut-outs and photographed them.

The joke misfired. Not only Elsie's parents believed them, but also psychic experts, so that the girls dared not confess the truth . . . until 1983, when Elsie, now an old lady, finally admitted what had happened.

WORDSEARCH

Look up, down, across, backwards and forwards as well as diagonally for the words below:

DRAGON — GIANT — WITCH — WIZARD — GHOST — VAMPIRE — SPOOK — GOBLIN — MONSTER — IMP — FAIRY — WEREWOLF.

```
W   I   Z   A   R   D   E   Q   W
G   A   V   S   N   R   L   T   E
I   P   Y   R   I   A   F   S   R
A   I   S   P   L   G   P   O   E
N   D   M   O   B   O   B   H   W
T   A   W   P   O   N   A   G   O
V   N   I   K   G   V   F   O   L
U   M   O   N   S   T   E   R   F
R   E   H   C   T   I   W   T   Y
```

Answers appear on page 48

What's a vampire's favourite fruit?
Blood oranges.

What do you call a very fast broomstick?
A brrm-brrrm-stick.

MAKING A FIREFLY LANTERN

Hang this lantern up in your garden, and when darkness falls it will look as if lots of fireflies are hovering there.

You'll need:
a tin can
a hammer
a thick nail
a block of wood which
will fit inside the tin can
a night-light
some strong wire
clean jam jar to fit inside the tin

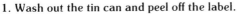

NOTE — BE CAREFUL, BECAUSE SHARP TINS CAN CUT YOU

1. Wash out the tin can and peel off the label.
2. Place the wood inside the tin can, and place it on its side on a firm surface.
3. Make holes all over the tin by bashing the nail part-way into the tin can, using the hammer. When you have made a hole, remove the nail and use it to make the next hole nearby.
4. Thread wire through holes at the top to make a handle.
5. Put the jam jar inside the tin, and a night-light inside the jar.

Now light the night-light. If you want a brighter light, cut away larger sections of the tin can. One variation could be to use tin strips to make star shapes in the tin. This needs strong wrists, so look for a helpful adult.

What did the monster tell himself before he went on stage?
It'll be all fright on the night!

SUPERSTITIONS

In olden days there were lots of strange things to frighten people. They did not know much about what made the world work, and when something terrible happened, like a fire caused by lightning, or the devastation of a hurricane or flood, he thought it must be a magical spirit's work. Things outside his understanding had to be caused by spirits, he believed.

Even today, people have a deep-rooted belief in good-luck charms and will stay on the safe side by respecting age-old superstitions, even though we now know that there are logical explanations for many of the things which we used to believe relied on good or bad luck. Here are some of them.

Touch Wood!
Have you ever touched wood to ward off bad luck? This dates from the earliest times in man's history. It was thought that spirits lived in trees, so men would touch a tree as they passed one, to let the spirit which lived there know that they needed its help.

Getting Married
A wedding is a time when you really do have to trust to the future! But to be on the safe side there are things you can do.

eg. 'Change the name but not the letter
Change for worse and not for better.'

This saying tells a bride that she must choose a husband whose surname begins with a different letter from her own — and it dates back to days when there were so few people around that to marry someone with the same initial as your own usually meant that you were marrying one of your own relatives.

Cats

People say that black cats bring luck .. but other people think that white cats are the lucky ones. It depends on where you live.

Cats are said to have nine lives not because they really do, but because they are so swift and agile that they seem to take awful risks. In fact, they are very careful creatures.

Horses and Horse-shoes

'One white foot — buy a horse,
Two white feet — try a horse,
Three white feet — look well about him,
Four white feet — do without him.'

The reasons for this saying are unknown — could it be that it was made up by somebody who just happened to have had a bad, white-footed horse at some time?

Horse-shoes should always be hung up with the ends at the top, or the good luck they bring will all run out, another saying goes.

Donkeys

If you look at a donkey's shoulders you will see that there are dark lines there. The superstition exists that these marks have been there ever since Christ rode a donkey into Jerusalem.

Swallows

The Romans believed that swallows were sacred to the gods of the household. Even today it is thought unlucky to kill one, and very lucky to have one nest in your house.

Sneezing

In the days when a sneeze could be the first sign of the plague, people thought it best to ward off any chance of sickness by saying 'God bless you' very hurriedly.

Even before that, men believed that sneezing was an explosion in the head, a message from the gods. Whether or not bad or good luck followed depended on when the sneeze happened. Maybe this old belief led to the following verse:

'Sneeze on Monday, sneeze for danger,
Sneeze on Tuesday, kiss a stranger,
Sneeze on Wednesday, get a letter,
Sneeze on Thursday, something better,
Sneeze on Friday, sneeze for sorrow,
Sneeze on Saturday, see your true love
tomorrow,
Sneeze on Sunday, dreams come true,
And you'll be happy all week through.'

Hiccups

'Hiccup, hiccup, go away,
Come again another day.
Hiccup, hiccup, when I bake
I'll give you a butter cake.'

As most attacks of the hiccups last only a few hours it is unlikely that any bout of them would last longer than the next baking session.

Nails

White specks on the nails couldn't be explained away, so they were taken as a sign of magic. It was said that it was a sign that you were going to receive a present . . . but you had to wait until the white speck grew to the end of the nail and was cut off.

'A gift on the finger
Is sure to linger
But on the thumb
Will never come.'

MAKING A SKELETON COSTUME

This is easy to make and just as effective as anything you can hire or buy.

You'll need:
*a white paper bag, big enough to fit on your head
black tights and jersey
sheets of strong white paper
needle and thread
scissors
black felt-tipped pen*

Copy the bones from this page on to the white paper so that they will fit your own arms, legs and body. Cut them out.

Stitch them to the tights and jersey, so that they can be seen all at once from the front.

Make a skull-like head from the paper bag by cutting round holes for the eye sockets and drawing a widely-grinning, toothy mouth on it. Add two dots for nostrils.

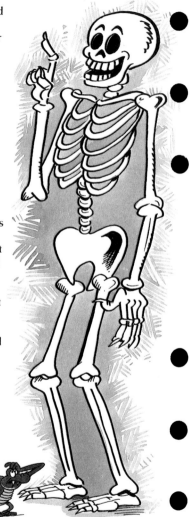

A CODED MESSAGE

The way this code has been worked out is quite easy. The message is a four-lined rhyme. Each line is separated from the others by a row of stars, and has its own code-breaker. But which of the numbered code-breakers goes with each line? The code-breakers work like this: If the first number is 2, look along a line to see what the second letter is and write it down. Then look at the next number (say 4) count along to the fourth letter from the start and write that down too — and so on until the end.

If you use the wrong code-breaker for a line it won't make sense. The answer to this is over the page.

I R F Y A C O U P W E I J S H N T L Y O P I L D O

✡ ✡ ✡ ✡ ✡ ✡

L B E I M V E A R N D U T O H R S I B W A V E X G

✡ ✡ ✡ ✡ ✡ ✡

K A L F E T G H A N D S O P R I V D E L J E D O R

✡ ✡ ✡ ✡ ✡ ✡

T I R C L U N H A M O P L Q I W I N V Y E T D A N

Code-breakers

1) 3   6   7   9   13   15   19   21

2) 1   3   4   7   8   10   12   14   15   17   20

3) 3   5   6   9   12   14   16   18   19   25

4) 1   4   6   7   8   10   11   13   15   16   18   22   23

What did the little ghost's teacher say to him?
Spook when you're spooken to!

ANSWERS TO PUZZLES

WORDSEARCH

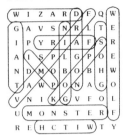

THE JOURNEY OF PEGASUS

THE FROG BOX

CROSSWORD PUZZLE

SPOOKY MAZE

The Coded Message 1st line — Code-breaker 2. 2nd line — Code-breaker 4. 3rd line — Code-breaker 3. 4th line — Code-breaker 1. If you wish to live and thrive, let a spider run alive.

Word Ladders Black, slack, slick, slice, spice, spine, shine, whine, white.

Witches' Saucepans Cauldrons — we made nod, nor, lad, cad, car, rod and don.

Coded Message If you wish to live and thrive, let a spider run alive